Contents

TRADITIONAL ENGLISH BISCUITS

Prep Time: 20 mins - **Total Time:** 40 mins

Servings per Recipe: 24

NUTRITIONALR VALUE

Calories73 kcal, Fat 4.1 g, Carbohydrates 8.2g, Protein 0.8 g, Cholesterol 19 mg, Sodium 118 mgw

INGREDIENTS

- 1/2 C. butter, softened
- 2 tbsp cornstarch
- 3/8 C. white sugar
- 1/4 tsp salt
- 1 tsp vanilla extract
- 1/4 C. rolled oats
- 1 egg yolk
- 1 C. self-rising flour

DIRECTIONS

Step 1

Set your oven to 375 degrees F before doing anything else and lightly, grease the cookie sheets.

Step 2

In a bowl, add the butter and sugar and beat till light and fluffy.

Step 3

Add the egg yolk and vanilla extract and beat well.

Step 4

In another bowl, sift together the flour, cornstarch and salt.

Step 5

Add the flour mixture into the butter mixture and mix till a dough forms.

Step 6

Make about 1/2-inch 20-24 small balls and roll each ball in the oats.

Step 7

Arrange onto the prepared cookie sheets about 2 inches apart.

Step 8

Cook in the oven for about 15-20 minutes.

CARAWAY LEMON BISCUITS

Prep Time: 50 mins **- Total Time:** 1 hr

Servings per Recipe: 12

NUTRITIONALR VALUE

Calories558 kcal, Fat 27.7 g, Carbohydrates 70g, Protein 8 g, Cholesterol 47 mg, Sodium 81 mg

INGREDIENTS

- 5 1/2 C. all-purpose flour

- 3 eggs

- 1 1/2 tsp lemon zest

- 3 tbsp milk

- 1 1/2 C. white sugar

- 3 tbsp caraway seed

- 1 1/2 tsp baking powder

- 1 1/2 C. shortening

DIRECTIONS

Step 1

Set your oven to 375 degrees F before doing anything else and line the cookie sheets with the parchment papers.

Step 2

In a large bowl, mix together the flour, baking powder and sugar.

Step 3

With a pastry cutter, cut the butter and mix till a coarse crumb forms.

Step 4

In another bowl, add the eggs, milk, seeds and lemon zest and beat well.

Step 5

Add the milk mixture into the flour mixture and mix till smooth.

Step 6

Place the dough onto floured surface and roll to 1/4-inch thickness.

Step 7

With a 2-inch round biscuit cutter, cut the dough into biscuits and arrange onto the prepared cookie sheets.

Step 8

Cook in the oven for about 7-10 minutes.

PARTY BISCUITS

Prep Time: 15 mins - **Total Time:** 40 mins

Servings per Recipe: 6

NUTRITIONALR VALUE

Calories286 kcal, Fat 7.7 g, Carbohydrates 47.9g, Protein 7.4 g, Cholesterol 3 mg, Sodium 272 mg

INGREDIENTS

- 1 1/2 C. all-purpose flour

- 1/3 C. honey

- 1/2 C. nonfat dry milk powder

- 3 tbsp canola oil

- 2 tsp baking powder

- 1/2 tsp vanilla extract

- 1 tsp ground cardamom

- 1 tbsp turbinado sugar

- 1/8 tsp salt

- 1/3 C. warm milk

DIRECTIONS

Step 1

Set your oven to 425 degrees F before doing anything else and lightly, grease a cookie sheet.

Step 2

In a bowl, mix together the flour, dry milk powder, baking powder, cardamom and salt.

Step 3

In another bowl, mix together the warm milk, honey, oil, and vanilla extract.

Step 4

Add the milk mixture into the flour mixture and mix till a dough forms.

Step 5

Place the dough onto a floured surface and gently pat into a 9x3-inch rectangle.

Step 6

With a sharp knife, cut the dough into 3 (3-inch) squares.

Step 7

Cut each square on the diagonal to make 6 triangles, and arrange the triangles onto the prepared cookie sheet.

Step 8

Cook in the oven for about 6 minutes.

Step 9

Remove from the oven and sprinkle the tops of the biscuits with the turbinado sugar.

Step 10

Cook in the oven for about 8 minutes more.

WONDERFUL BISCUITS

Prep Time: 15 mins **- Total Time:** 2 hrs

Servings per Recipe: 12

NUTRITIONALR VALUE

Calories79 kcal, Fat 4.7 g, Carbohydrates 8.2g, Protein 1.1 g, Cholesterol 0 mg, Sodium 156 mg

INGREDIENTS

- 1 C. Herman Sourdough Starter

- 1/4 tsp salt

- 1 C. all-purpose flour

- 1/4 C. vegetable oil

- 1/4 tsp baking soda

- 2 tsp baking powder

DIRECTIONS

Step 1

Lightly, grease a cookie sheet.

Step 2

Bring Herman Starter to room temperature.

Step 3

Stir together flour, baking soda, baking soda and salt.

Step 4

Add the flour mixture and oil into Herman Starter and stir till a soft dough forms.

Step 5

Place the dough onto a lightly floured surface and knead till smooth.

Step 6

Roll the dough and with a biscuit cutter, cut the biscuits.

Step 7

Place the biscuits onto the prepared cookie sheet.

Step 8

Cover the cookie sheet and keep aside in the warm place for about 1 hour.

Step 9

Set your oven to 350 degrees F.

Step 10

Cook in the oven for about 30 minutes.

BISCUITS AUSTRALIAN STYLE

Prep Time: 15 mins **- Total Time:** 1 hr 20 mins

Servings per Recipe: 10

NUTRITIONALR VALUE

Calories196 kcal, Fat 3.9 g, Carbohydrates 33.7g, Protein 6 g, Cholesterol 1 mg, Sodium 475 mg

INGREDIENTS

- 1 1/2 tsp active dry yeast

- 3/4 C. milk

- 1 tsp white sugar

- 2 tbsp vegetable oil

- 1 C. warm water

- 1/4 C. cornmeal

- 3 C. unbleached flour

- 2 tsp salt

DIRECTIONS

Step 1

In a small bowl, dissolve the sugar and yeast in warm water and keep aside for about 10 minutes.

Step 2

To make crumpet rings, cut the aluminum foil into 7x12-inch pieces.

Step 3

Fold in half lengthwise and then in thirds, making 6 layers.

Step 4

Form into a 3 1/2-inch diameter circle and tape shut on the outside.

Step 5

In a large bowl, mix together the flour and salt.

Step 6

Add the milk, oil and yeast mixture and beat well till smooth.

Step 7

Cover with plastic wrap and keep in a warm place for about 60 minutes.

Step 8

Lightly grease the inside of the crumpet rings and then, dip the rings in cornmeal.

Step 9

Heat a frying pan on medium-low heat and sprinkle with the cornmeal.

Step 10

Place the rings on the frying pan and deflate the mixture by stirring.

Step 11

Place 1/4 C. of the mixture into each ring and cook slowly for about 10 minutes.

Step 12

Carefully remove the rings and flip the biscuits and cook for about 8 minutes.

BISCUITS FOR AUTUMN

Prep Time: 30 mins **- Total Time:** 50 mins

Servings per Recipe: 36

NUTRITIONALR VALUE

Calories 62 kcal, Fat 2.7 g, Carbohydrates 8.5g, Protein 1 g, Cholesterol 7 mg, Sodium 92 mg

INGREDIENTS

- 2 1/2 C. all-purpose flour

- 1/4 tsp ground cinnamon

- 3 tbsp packed brown sugar

- 1/4 tsp ground ginger

- 1 tbsp baking powder

- 1/2 C. butter, sliced

- 1/2 tsp salt

- 2 C. pumpkin puree

- 1/4 tsp ground nutmeg

DIRECTIONS

Step 1

Set your oven to 400 degrees F before doing anything else and grease a large cookie sheet.

Step 2

In a large bowl, mix together the flour, baking powder, brown sugar and spices.

Step 3

With a pastry cutter, cut the butter and mix till a coarse crumb forms.

Step 4

Add the pumpkin puree and mix till a soft dough forms.

Step 5

Place the dough onto floured surface and roll to 1/2-inch thickness.

Step 6

With a biscuit cutter, cut the dough into 2-inch round biscuits and arrange onto a cookie sheet.

Step 7

Cook in the oven for about 15-20 minutes.

HASH BROWN FULL BREAKFAST MUFFINS

Prep Time: 20 mins **- Total Time:** 50 mins

Servings per Recipe: 12

NUTRITIONALR VALUE

Calories 224 kcal, Fat   18.3 g, Carbohydrates 8.6g, Protein 11.2 g, Cholesterol 114 mg, Sodium 413 mg

INGREDIENTS

- 12 links Johnsonville(R) Original breakfast
- 6 eggs, lightly beaten
- sausage
- 2 C. shredded 4-cheese Mexican blend cheese
- 3 C. frozen country style shredded hash
- 1/4 C. chopped red bell pepper
- brown potatoes, thawed
- chopped fresh chives
- 3 tbsp butter, melted
- 1/8 tsp salt
- 1/8 tsp pepper

DIRECTIONS

Step 1

Set your oven to 400 degrees F before doing anything else and grease 12 cups of a muffin pan.

Step 2

Prepare the sausage according to the package's directions.

Step 3

Keep aside to cool slightly and cut into 1/2-inch pieces.

Step 4

In a bowl, mix together the hash browns, butter, salt and pepper.

Step 5

Transfer the mixture into the prepared muffin cups evenly and press onto the sides and bottom of the cups.

Step 6

Cook in the oven for about 12 minutes.

Step 7

Remove from the oven and divide the sausage pieces into muffin cups evenly.

Step 8

In a bowl, mix together the eggs, cheese and bell pepper.

Step 9

Place the egg mixture into muffin cups and top with the chives.

Step 10

Cook in the oven for about 13-15 minutes more.

GEORGIAN MUFFINS

Prep Time: 25 mins **- Total Time:** 50 mins

Servings per Recipe: 16

NUTRITIONALR VALUE

Calories351 kcal, Fat 18.2 g, Carbohydrates 44.3g, Protein 3.6 g, Cholesterol 35 mg,Sodium 238 mg

INGREDIENTS

- 3 C. all-purpose flour
- 2 C. white sugar

- 1 tbsp ground cinnamon

- 2 C. peeled, pitted, and chopped peaches

- 1 tsp baking soda

- 1 tsp salt

- 1 1/4 C. vegetable oil

- 3 eggs, lightly beaten

DIRECTIONS

Step 1

Set your oven to 400 degrees F before doing anything else and lightly, grease 16 cups of the muffin pans.

Step 2

In a large bowl, mix together the flour, cinnamon, baking soda and salt.

Step 3

In another bowl, add the oil, eggs and sugar and beat till smooth.

Step 4

Add the oil mixture into the flour mixture and mix till just moistened.

Step 5

Fold in the peaches.

Step 6

Transfer the mixture into the prepared muffin cups evenly.

Step 7

Cook in the oven for about 25 minutes or till a toothpick inserted in the center comes out clean.

Step 8

Remove from the oven and cool for about 10 minutes before turning out onto wire rack to cool completely.

CITRUS BOOST MUFFINS

Prep Time: 10 mins - **Total Time:** 40 mins

Servings per Recipe: 12

NUTRITIONALR VALUE

Calories176 kcal, Fat 6.8 g, Carbohydrates 26.3g, Protein 2.8 g, Cholesterol 16 mg, Sodium 225 mg

INGREDIENTS

- 2 C. all-purpose flour
- 1/3 C. vegetable oil
- 1/2 C. white sugar
- 1 egg
- 3 tsp baking powder
- 1 tbsp orange zest
- 1/2 tsp salt
- 3/4 C. orange juice

DIRECTIONS

Step 1

Set your oven to 400 degrees F before doing anything else and lightly, grease 12 cups of a muffin pan.

Step 2

In a bowl, mix together the flour, sugar, baking powder, orange peel and salt.

Step 3

In another bowl, add the orange juice, oil and egg and beat till well combined.

Step 4

Add the flour mixture and mix till just moistened.

Step 5

Transfer the mixture into the prepared muffin cups about 2/3 full.

Step 6

Cook in the oven for about 20-25 minutes or till a toothpick inserted in the center comes out clean.

OATMEAL AND CINNAMON COOKIES

Prep Time: 10 mins **- Total Time:** 2 hrs

Servings per Recipe: 24

NUTRITIONALR VALUE

Calories218 kcal, Carbohydrates 32.3 g, Cholesterol 36 mg, Fat 8.8 gFiber 1.4 g, Protein 3 g, Sodium 213 mg

INGREDIENTS

- 1 C. butter, softened

- 1 tsp baking soda

- 1 C. white sugar

- 1 tsp salt

- 1 C. packed brown sugar

- 1 1/2 tsps ground cinnamon

- 2 eggs

- 3 C. quick cooking oats

- 1 tsp vanilla extract

- 2 C. all-purpose flour

DIRECTIONS

Step 1

Set your oven at 350 degrees F before doing anything else.

Step 2

Add a mixture of flour, salt, baking soda and cinnamon into a mixture of butter, vanilla, eggs, sugar and brown sugar before stirring in oats and forming balls out of this dough.

Step 3

Place these balls with some distance on a baking sheet.

Step 4

Bake everything in the preheated oven for about 10 minutes.

Step 5

Cool it down.

Step 6

Serve.

CHOCOLATE COOKIES

Prep Time: 15 mins **- Total Time:** 45 mins

Servings per Recipe: 60

NUTRITIONALR VALUE

Calories125 kcal, Carbohydrates 15.5 g, Cholesterol 18 mg, Fat 7.1 gFiber 1 g, Protein 1.5 g, Sodium 63 mg

INGREDIENTS

- 1 C. butter, softened

- 2/3 C. cocoa powder

- 1 1/2 C. white sugar

- 3/4 tsp baking soda

- 2 eggs

- 1/4 tsp salt

- 2 tsps vanilla extract

- 2 C. semisweet chocolate chips

- 2 C. all-purpose flour

- 1/2 C. chopped walnuts (optional)

DIRECTIONS

Step 1

Set your oven at 350 degrees F before doing anything else.

Step 2

Add a mixture of flour, cocoa, baking soda, and salt into a mixture of butter, sugar, eggs, and vanilla before stirring in some chocolate chips and walnuts.

Step 3

Pour spoonfuls of this mixture with some distance on a baking sheet.

Step 4

Bake everything in the preheated oven for about 10 minutes.

Step 5

Cool it down.

Step 6

Serve.

BUTTERY LEMON COOKIES

Prep Time: 15 mins **- Total Time:** 1 hr 05 mins

Servings per Recipe: 48

NUTRITIONALR VALUE

Calories90 kcal, Carbohydrates 12.4 g, Cholesterol 18 mg, Fat 4.1 g , Fiber 0.2 g, Protein 1.1 g, Sodium 81 mg

INGREDIENTS

- 3 C. all-purpose flour
- 2 eggs
- 1 tsp baking soda
- 1/4 C. lemon juice
- 1/2 tsp salt
- 1 lemon, zested
- 1 C. butter, softened
- 1/2 tsp vanilla extract
- 1 1/2 C. white sugar

DIRECTIONS

Step 1

Set your oven at 350 degrees F before doing anything else.

Step 2

Add a mixture of flour, baking soda, and salt into a mixture of butter, sugar, eggs (one at a time), lemon juice, lemon zest, and vanilla extract before cooling it down for thirty minutes.

Step 3

Pour spoonfuls of this mixture with some distance on a baking sheet.

Step 4

Bake everything in the preheated oven for about 8 minutes.

Step 5

Cool it down.

Step 6

Serve.

SIMPLE SUGAR MUFFINS

Prep Time: 10 mins **- Total Time:** 30 mins

Servings per Recipe: 12

NUTRITIONALR VALUE

Calories141 kcal, Fat 5.4 g, Carbohydrates 21g, Protein 2.5 g, Cholesterol 16 mg, Sodium 188 mg

INGREDIENTS

- 1 egg

- 1/2 C. white sugar

- 1/2 C. milk

- 2 tsp baking powder

- 1/4 C. vegetable oil

- 1/2 tsp salt

- 1 1/2 C. all-purpose flour, sifted

DIRECTIONS

Step 1

Set your oven to 400 degrees F before doing anything else and grease 12 cups of a muffin pan.

Step 2

In a bowl, add the egg and beat with a fork.

Step 3

Stir in the milk and oil.

Step 4

In another bowl, mix together the sugar, baking powder and salt.

Step 5

Add the egg mixture into flour mixture and stir till the mixture is just moistened.

Step 6

Transfer the mixture into the prepared muffin cups about 2/3 full.

Step 7

Cook in the oven for about 20-25 minutes or till a toothpick inserted in the center comes out clean.

- Whole Wheat Muffins

Prep Time: 10 mins - **Total Time:** 25 mins

Servings per Recipe: 16

NUTRITIONALR VALUE

Calories176 kcal, Fat 7.7 g, Carbohydrates 24.8g, Protein 3.7 g, Cholesterol 12 mg, Sodium 268 mg

INGREDIENTS

- 2 1/4 C. whole wheat flour

- 1 C. buttermilk

- 1/3 C. millet

- 1 egg, lightly beaten

- 1 tsp baking powder

- 1/2 C. vegetable oil

- 1 tsp baking soda

- 1/2 C. honey

- 1 tsp salt

DIRECTIONS

Step 1

Set your oven to 400 degrees F before doing anything else and lightly, grease 10 cups of a muffin pan.

Step 2

In a large bowl, mix together the whole wheat flour, millet flour, baking powder, baking soda and salt.

Step 3

In another bowl, mix together the buttermilk, egg, vegetable oil and honey.

Step 4

Add the buttermilk mixture into the flour mixture and mix till just moistened.

Step 5

Transfer the mixture into the prepared muffin cups evenly.

Step 6

Cook in the oven for about 15 minutes or till a toothpick inserted in the center comes out clean.

OCTOBER'S MUFFINS

Prep Time: 45 mins **- Total Time:** 1 hr 15 mins

Servings per Recipe: 18

NUTRITIONALR VALUE

Calories 304 kcal, Fat 14.6 g, Carbohydrates 40.9g, Protein 4.2 g, Cholesterol 49 mg, Sodium 284 mg

INGREDIENTS

- 3/4 C. brown sugar

- 1 C. butter, melted

- 3/4 C. white sugar

- 2 eggs, beaten

- 3 C. all-purpose flour

- 1 1/4 C. milk

- 1/2 tsp baking soda

- 1 C. chopped cranberries

- 1 tbsp baking powder

- 1 C. chopped, peeled apple

- 1/2 tsp salt

- 1/2 C. chopped dried figs

- 2 tsp ground cinnamon

- 3/4 C. chopped toasted hazelnuts

- 1/2 tsp ground nutmeg

- 1 tsp ground ginger

DIRECTIONS

Step 1

Set your oven to 375 degrees F before doing anything else and grease 18 cups of the muffin pans.

Step 2

In a large bowl, mix together the brown sugar, white sugar, flour, baking powder, baking soda, salt, cinnamon, nutmeg and ginger.

Step 3

Make a well in the center of the mixture.

Step 4

In the well, add the melted butter, milk and eggs and mix till smooth.

Step 5

Fold in the cranberries, apple, figs and hazelnuts.

Step 6

Transfer the mixture into the prepared muffin cups about 3/4 full.

Step 7

Cook in the oven for about 15-20 minutes or till a toothpick inserted in the center comes out clean.

EASY ALMOND RHUBARB MUFFINS

Prep Time: 10 mins **- Total Time:** 35 mins

Servings per Recipe: 12

NUTRITIONALR VALUE

Calories192 kcal, Fat 6.6 g, Carbohydrates 31g, Protein 3 g, Cholesterol 23 mg, Sodium 138 mg

INGREDIENTS

- 1/2 C. vanilla yogurt

- 1 C. diced rhubarb

- 2 tbsp butter, melted

- 1/4 C. brown sugar

- 2 tbsp vegetable oil

- 1/2 tsp ground cinnamon

- 1 egg

- 1/4 tsp ground nutmeg

- 1 1/3 C. all-purpose flour

- 1/4 C. crushed sliced almonds

- 3/4 C. brown sugar

- 2 tsp melted butter

- 1/2 tsp baking soda

- 1/4 tsp salt

DIRECTIONS

Step 1

Set your oven to 350 degrees F before doing anything else and lightly, grease 12 cups of a muffin pan.

Step 2

In a bowl, mix together the yogurt, 2 tbsp of the melted butter, oil and egg.

Step 3

In another large bowl, mix together the flour, 3/4 C. of the brown sugar, baking soda and salt.

Step 4

Add the yogurt mixture into the flour mixture and mix till just combined.

Step 5

Fold in the rhubarb.

Step 6

Transfer the mixture into the prepared muffin cups about 2/3 full.

Step 7

In a small bowl, mix together 1/4 C. of the brown sugar, cinnamon, nutmeg, almonds and 2 tsp of the melted butter.

Step 8

Place the mixture over the tops of the muffins and press down slightly.

Step 9

Cook in the oven for about 25 minutes or till a toothpick inserted in the center comes out clean.

Step 10

Remove from the oven and cool for about 15 minutes before turning out onto wire rack to cool completely.

IVY LEAGUE MUFFINS

Prep Time: 10 mins - **Total Time:** 30 mins

Servings per Recipe: 12

NUTRITIONALR VALUE

Calories215 kcal, Fat 6.4 g, Carbohydrates 38g, Protein 3.8 g, Cholesterol 18 mg, Sodium 366 mg

INGREDIENTS

- 1 egg

- 1 tsp ground cinnamon

- 1 1/3 C. mashed ripe banana

- 1 C. quick cooking oats

- 3/4 C. packed brown sugar

- 1/2 C. semisweet chocolate chips

- 1/3 C. applesauce

- 1/2 C. chopped walnuts

- 1 tsp vanilla extract

- 1 C. all-purpose flour

- 1/2 tsp baking soda

- 2 tsp baking powder

- 1 1/4 tsp salt

DIRECTIONS

Step 1

Set your oven to 350 degrees F before doing anything else and lightly, grease 12 cups of a muffin pan.

Step 2

In a large bowl, add the egg, banana, brown sugar, applesauce and vanilla and beat till well combined.

Step 3

In another bowl, sift together the flour, baking soda, baking powder, salt and cinnamon.

Step 4

Add the flour mixture and oatmeal into banana mixture and gently, stir to combine.

Step 5

Fold in the chocolate chips and walnuts.

Step 6

Transfer the mixture into the prepared muffin cups evenly.

Step 7

Cook in the oven for about 15-20 minutes or till a toothpick inserted in the center comes out clean.

Step 8

Remove from the oven and keep on wire rack to cool completely.

WEDNESDAY'S MUFFINS

Prep Time: 10 mins - **Total Time:** 35 mins

Servings per Recipe: 12

NUTRITIONALR VALUE

Calories187 kcal, Fat 5.8 g, Carbohydrates 32.3g, Protein 2.6 g, Cholesterol 29 mg, Sodium 275 mg

INGREDIENTS

- 1 1/2 C. all-purpose flour

- 3/4 C. white sugar

- 1 tsp baking powder

- 1 egg

- 1 tsp baking soda

- 1/3 C. butter, melted

- 1/2 tsp salt

- 3 large bananas, mashed

DIRECTIONS

Step 1

Set your oven to 350 degrees F before doing anything else and lightly, grease 12 cups of a muffin pan.

Step 2

In a bowl, sift together the flour, baking powder, baking soda and salt.

Step 3

In another large bowl, add the bananas, sugar, egg and melted butter and beat till well combined.

Step 4

Add the flour mixture and mix till smooth.

Step 5

Transfer the mixture into the prepared muffin cups evenly.

Step 6

Cook in the oven for about 25-30 minutes or till a toothpick inserted in the center comes out clean.

SOUTHWESTERN MUFFINS

Prep Time: 15 mins **- Total Time:** 40 mins

Servings per Recipe: 12

NUTRITIONALR VALUE

Calories195 kcal, Fat 8.6 g, Carbohydrates 26.6g, Protein 3.2 g, Cholesterol 37 mg, Sodium 358 mg

INGREDIENTS

- 1 C. all-purpose flour
- 1 C. buttermilk
- 1 C. yellow cornmeal
- 1/2 C. butter, melted
- 1/2 C. white sugar
- 1 egg, beaten
- 2 tsp baking powder
- 1 tsp salt

DIRECTIONS

Step 1

Set your oven to 400 degrees F before doing anything else and lightly, grease 12 cups of a muffin pan.

Step 2

In a large bowl, mix together the flour, cornmeal, sugar, baking powder and salt.

Step 3

Add the buttermilk, butter and egg; mix till well combined.

Step 4

Transfer the mixture into the prepared muffin cups evenly.

Step 5

Cook in the oven for about 12-15 minutes or till a toothpick inserted in the center comes out clean.

Step 6

Remove from the oven and cool for about 15 minutes before turning out onto wire rack to cool completely.

THYME MUSHROOM AND FETA MUFFINS

Prep Time: 15 mins **- Total Time:** 35 mins

Servings per Recipe: 6

NUTRITIONALR VALUE

Calories94 kcal, Fat 4.5 g, Carbohydrates 7.8g, Protein 5.6 g, Cholesterol 99 mg, Sodium 133 mg

INGREDIENTS

- cooking spray

- 1/4 C. chopped onion

- 1 C. cooked quinoa

- 1/2 tsp dried thyme

- 3 large eggs, beaten

- salt and ground black pepper to taste

- 1/4 C. crumbled feta cheese

- 1/4 C. sliced mushrooms

DIRECTIONS

Step 1

Set your oven to 400 degrees F before doing anything else and lightly, grease 6 cups of a muffin pan.

Step 2

In a large bowl, add the quinoa, eggs, feta cheese, mushrooms, onion, thyme, salt and pepper and beat till well combined.

Step 3

Transfer the mixture into the prepared muffin cups about halfway full.

Step 4

Cook in the oven for about 20-30 minutes or till a toothpick inserted in the center comes out clean.

SPICY CARDAMOM COOKIES

Prep Time: 15 mins **- Total Time:** 3 hrs

Servings per Recipe: 36

NUTRITIONALR VALUE

Calories 284 kcal, Carbohydrates 53.9 g, Cholesterol 21 mg, Fat 6.3 g , Fiber 1.1 g, Protein 3.7 g, Sodium 213 mg

INGREDIENTS

- 1/2 C. molasses

- 1 tsp ground cloves

- 1/4 C. honey

- 1 tsp ground ginger

- 1/4 C. shortening

- 2 tsps anise extract

- 1/4 C. margarine

- 2 tsps ground cinnamon

- 2 eggs

- 1 1/2 tsps baking soda

- 4 C. all-purpose flour

- 1 tsp ground black pepper

- 3/4 C. white sugar

- 1/2 tsp salt

- 1/2 C. brown sugar

- 1 C. confectioners' sugar for dusting

- 1 1/2 tsps ground cardamom

- 1 tsp ground nutmeg

DIRECTIONS

Step 1

Set your oven at 350 degrees F before doing anything else.

Step 2

Add a mixture of flour, white sugar, brown sugar, cardamom, nutmeg, cloves, ginger, anise, cinnamon, baking soda, pepper, and salt into a melted mixture of molasses, honey, shortening, eggs and margarine before forming small sized balls out of it.

Step 3

Place these balls with some distance on a baking sheet.

Step 4

Bake everything in the preheated oven for about 15 minutes.

BANANA COCONUTS AND QUINOA

Prep Time: 10 mins **- Total Time:** 50 mins

Servings per Recipe: 24

NUTRITIONALR VALUE

Calories188 kcal, Carbohydrates 27.6 g, Cholesterol 0 mg, Fat 7.6 g , Fiber 2.7 g, Protein 4.3 g, Sodium 274 mg

INGREDIENTS

- 2/3 C. water

- 1/2 C. peanut butter

- 1/3 C. quinoa

- 1 tsp vanilla extract

- 1 C. shredded coconut

- 1 tsp salt

- 1 C. rolled oats

- 1 tsp baking soda

- 1 C. all-purpose flour

- 1 tsp baking powder

- 3/4 C. brown sugar

- 3/4 C. semisweet chocolate chips

- 2 ripe bananas, crushed

- 1/2 C. applesauce

DIRECTIONS

Step 1

Set your oven at 350 degrees F before doing anything else.

Step 2

Bring a mixture of quinoa and water to boil, and cook for 20 minutes over medium heat.

Step 3

Combine cooked quinoa, coconut, oats, flour, brown sugar, baking soda, crushed bananas, vanilla, applesauce, peanut butter, salt and baking powder in a large sized bowl before stirring in some chocolate chips.

Step 4

Pour spoonfuls of this mixture with some distance on a baking sheet.

Step 5

Bake everything in the preheated oven for about 25 minutes.

Step 6

Cool it down.

Step 7

Serve.

CHOCOLATE YOGURT COOKIES

Prep Time: 10 mins - **Total Time:** 22 mins

Servings per Recipe: 36

NUTRITIONALR VALUE

Calories115 kcal, Fat 5.5 g, Carbohydrates 16.6g, Protein 1.2 g, Cholesterol 1 mg, Sodium 68 mg

INGREDIENTS

- 1/2 C. packed brown sugar

- 1 3/4 C. all-purpose flour

- 1/2 C. white sugar

- 1/2 tsp baking soda

- 1/4 C. margarine or butter

- 1/2 tsp salt

- 1/4 C. shortening

- 2 C. semisweet chocolate chips

- 1/2 C. plain nonfat yogurt

- 2 tsps vanilla extract

DIRECTIONS

Step 1

Coat some baking sheets with some oil then set your oven to 375 degrees before doing anything else.

Step 2

Get a bowl, combine and cream the following: shortening, brown sugar, margarine, and white sugar. Stir the mix until it is fluffy then combine in the vanilla and yogurt.

Step 3

Slowly work in the salt, baking soda, flour. Work the mix completely then add in the chocolate chips.

Step 4

Layer dollops of the mix on the baking sheets and cook everything in the oven for 12 mins. Let the cookies cool completely then serve them.

Step 5

Enjoy.

TRADITIONAL CHRISTMAS& HOLIDAY COOKIES

Prep Time: 20 mins **- Total Time:** 1 hr

Servings per Recipe: 24

NUTRITIONALR VALUE

Calories79 kcal, Fat 4.3 g, Carbohydrates 9.5g, Protein 0.7 g, Cholesterol 1 mg, Sodium 28 mg

INGREDIENTS

- 1/4 C. white sugar

- 3/4 tsp ground cinnamon

- 1 sheet frozen puff pastry, thawed

- 1/8 tsp ground cardamom

- 1 tbsp butter, melted

- water

- 1/3 C. white sugar

DIRECTIONS

Step 1

Set your oven to 375 degrees F before doing anything else and line a baking sheet with parchment paper.

Step 2

Spread 1/4 C. of the sugar over a smooth surface.

Step 3

Unfold the puff pastry over sugar and roll out to a 15x10-inch rectangle.

Step 4

In a bowl, mix together the remaining sugar, cinnamon and cardamom.

Step 5

Coat the pastry with the melted butter evenly and top with the cinnamon mixture evenly.

Step 6

Starting from the long edge of the pastry, roll pastry tightly around filling, stopping in the middle.

Step 7

Repeat with the opposite edge, meeting the first roll.

Step 8

With your wet fingers press gently so the two rolled edges stay together.

Step 9

Refrigerate for about 5-10 minutes.

Step 10

Cut the pastry into 1/4-inch slices and place onto prepared baking sheet in a single layer about 1-inch apart.

Step 11

Cook everything in the oven for about 12 minutes.

NEW ENGLAND APPLE COOKIES

Prep Time: 30 mins - **Total Time:** 1 hr 18 mins

Servings per Recipe: 60

NUTRITIONALR VALUE

Calories77 kcal, Fat 2.8 g, Carbohydrates 12.7g, Protein 0.9 g, Cholesterol 7 mg, Sodium 55 mg

INGREDIENTS

- 2 C. all-purpose flour

- 1 egg, beaten

- 1 tsp baking soda

- 1 C. chopped walnuts

- 1 tsp ground cinnamon

- 1 C. chopped apples

- 1 tsp ground cloves

- 1 C. raisins

- 1/2 tsp ground nutmeg

- 2/3 C. confectioners' sugar

- 1/2 tsp salt

- 1 tbsp milk

- 1/2 C. softened butter

- 1 1/2 C. packed brown sugar

DIRECTIONS

Step 1

Set your oven to 350 degrees F before doing anything else and line the cookie sheets with parchment papers.

Step 2

In a large bowl, sift together the flour, baking soda, spices and salt.

Step 3

In another bowl, add the butter and beat till fluffy and light.

Step 4

Add the egg and sugar and mix till well combined.

Step 5

Add the egg mixture into the flour mixture and mix till well combined.

Step 6

Fold in the apples, raisins and walnuts.

Step 7

With a teaspoon, place the mixture onto the prepared cookie sheets in a single layer about 1 1/2-inches apart.

Step 8

Cook everything in the oven for about 12-14 minutes.

Step 9

Remove everything from the oven and keep aside on wire racks to cool completely.

Step 10

Meanwhile for the glaze in a small bowl, mix together the remaining ingredients.

Step 11

Pour the glaze over the cookies and serve.

CHEWY COOKIES 101

Prep Time: 20 mins - **Total Time:** 40 mins

Servings per Recipe: 36

NUTRITIONALR VALUE

Calories90 kcal, Fat 5.4 g, Carbohydrates 9.4g, Protein 1.5 g, Cholesterol 10 mg, Sodium 50 mg

INGREDIENTS

- 1C. sifted all-purpose flour

- 2 eggs

- 1 tsp baking powder

- 1 C. chopped walnuts

- 1/2 tsp salt

- 1 C. apples - peeled, cored and finely

- 1 tsp ground cinnamon

- diced

- 1/2 tsp ground nutmeg

- 1 C. rolled oats

- 1/2 C. shortening

- 3/4 C. white sugar

DIRECTIONS

Step 1

Set your oven to 350 degrees F before doing anything else.

Step 2

In a large bowl, mix together the flour, baking powder, cinnamon, nutmeg and salt.

Step 3

In another bowl, add the shortening and white sugar and beat till smooth and creamy.

Step 4

Add the eggs and beat till well combined.

Step 5

Add the egg mixture into the flour mixture and mix till well combined.

Step 6

Fold in the oats, apples and walnuts.

Step 7

With a spoon, place the mixture onto the cookie sheets in a single layer about 2-inches apart.

Step 8

Cook everything in the oven for about 12-15 minutes.

Step 9

Remove everything from the oven and keep it all on wire racks to cool completely.

LEMON PUDDING CAKE

Prep Time: 30 mins **- Total Time:** 35 mins

Servings per Recipe: 12

NUTRITIONALR VALUE

Calories425 kcal, Fat 13 g, Carbohydrates 74.1g, Protein 4.7 g, Cholesterol 73 mg, Sodium 441 mg

INGREDIENTS

- 4 eggs

- 1/2 C. lemon juice

- 1 (3 oz.) package instant lemon pudding

- 3 C. sifted confectioners' sugar mix

- 1/4 C. confectioners' sugar for dusting

- 1/3 C. vegetable oil

- 1 (18.25 oz.) package lemon cake mix

- 3/4 C. water

DIRECTIONS

Step 1

Set your oven to 350 degrees F before doing anything else and grease and flour a bundt pan.

Step 2

In a bowl, add the eggs and beat till thick.

Step 3

Add the cake mix, pudding mix, oil and water and with an electric mixer, beat on medium speed for about 5 minutes.

Step 4

Transfer the mixture into the prepared pan and cook in the oven for about 50 minutes or till a toothpick inserted in the center comes out clean.

Step 5

Meanwhile for glaze in a mix together the 3 C. of the confectioner's sugar and lemon juice and heat till boiling.

Step 6

Pour the hot glaze over the hot cake and keep aside for about 1 hour to cool.

Step 7

Carefully, invert the cake over the serving plate.

Step 8

Serve with a dusting of the confectioner's sugar.

YELLOW VANILLA CAKE

Prep Time: 30 mins **- Total Time:** 1 hr 30 mins

Servings per Recipe: 12

NUTRITIONALR VALUE

Calories562 kcal, Fat 29.9 g, Carbohydrates 59.2g, Protein 5.6 g, Cholesterol 83 mg, Sodium 476 mg

INGREDIENTS

- 1 C. chopped walnuts
- 1/2 C. cranberry
- 1 (18.25 oz.) package yellow cake mix
- 1/2 C. butter
- 1 (3.4 oz.) package instant vanilla
- 1/4 C. water
- pudding mix
- 1 C. white sugar
- 4 eggs
- 1/2 C. apple juice
- 1/2 C. water
- 1/2 C. vegetable oil

DIRECTIONS

Step 1

Set your oven to 325 degrees F before doing anything else and grease and flour a 10-inch bundt pan.

Step 2

In the bottom of the prepared pan, spread the walnuts.

Step 3

In a large bowl, mix together the pudding mix and cake mix.

Step 4

Add the eggs, oil, 1/2 C. of the cranberry juice and 1/2 C. of the water and mix till well combined.

Step 5

Transfer the mixture over walnuts evenly and cook in the oven for about 60 minutes or till a toothpick inserted in the center comes out clean.

Step 6

For glaze in a pan, mix together the butter, 1 C. of the sugar and 1/4 C. of the water on medium heat.

Step 7

Bring to a boil and boil for about 5 minutes, stirring continuously.

Step 8

Remove from the heat and immediately, stir in the apple juice.

Step 9

Remove the cake from the oven and keep aside for about 10 minutes.

Step 10

Cot the top and sides of the cake with the glaze evenly.

Step 11

Let the cake absorb the glaze completely, then again coat with the remaining glaz

PINEAPPLE, ORANGE, AND VANILLA YELLOW CAKE

Prep Time: 30 mins - **Total Time:**9 hrs 55 mins

Servings per Recipe: 12

NUTRITIONALR VALUE

Calories562 kcal, Fat 29.9 g, Carbohydrates 59.2g, Protein 5.6 g, Cholesterol 83 mg, Sodium 476 mg

INGREDIENTS

- 1 (18.25 oz.) package yellow cake mix

- 1 (3.5 oz.) package instant vanilla pudding

- 8 oz. cream cheese

- mix

- 1 1/2 C. confectioners' sugar

- 1 (8 oz.) container frozen whipped

- 1 (20 oz.) can crushed pineapple with

- topping, thawed

- juice

- 2 (8 oz.) cans mandarin oranges,

- drained

DIRECTIONS

Step 1

Mix and bake the cake mix as per package instruction for 2 (8-9-inch) round layers.

Step 2

Keep aside the layers to cool and then split each layer in half so as to have 4 layers.

Step 3

In a large bowl, add the cream cheese and beat till soft.

Step 4

Slowly, mix in the confectioners' sugar.

Step 5

Add the pineapple with juice and the drained mandarin oranges, reserving about 5 mandarin orange slices and mix till well combined.

Step 6

Mix in the dry pudding mix and fold in the whipped topping.

Step 7

Arrange one cake layer onto a cake plate cut side up.

Step 8

Spread frosting over the layer and place another layer cut side down on the first one.

Step 9

Top with the frosting.

Step 10

Repeat till all the layers are used, spreading all the frosting on top and sides of cake.

Step 11

Garnish with the reserved mandarin orange slices.

Step 12

Refrigerate for overnight before serving.

LAYEREDCAKE 101

Prep Time: 5 mins **- Total Time:** 2 hrs

Servings per Recipe: 12

NUTRITIONALR VALUE

Calories465 kcal, Fat 28.9 g, Carbohydrates 46.3g, Protein 4.4 g, Cholesterol 78 mg, Sodium 309 mg

INGREDIENTS

- Cake:

- Frosting:

- 1 (18.25 oz.) package moist white cake mix

- 2 C. heavy cream

- 1 tsp instant coffee powder

- 1/4 C. confectioners' sugar

- 1/4 C. coffee

- 2 tbsp coffee flavored liqueur

- 1 tbsp coffee flavored liqueur

- Garnish:

- Filling:

- 2 tbsp unsweetened cocoa powder

- 1 (8 oz.) container mascarpone cheese

- 1 (1 oz.) square semisweet chocolate

- 1/2 C. confectioners' sugar

- 2 tbsp coffee flavored liqueur

DIRECTIONS

Step 1

Set your oven to 350 degrees F before doing anything else and grease and flour 3 (9-inch) cake pans.

Step 2

Mix the cake mix according to package directions.

Step 3

Divide two thirds of the mixture between 2 pans.

Step 4

In the remaining mixture, stir in the instant coffee and transfer into the third pan.

Step 5

Cook in the oven for about 20-25 minutes or till a toothpick inserted in the center comes out clean.

Step 6

Let the cakes cool in the pans for about 10 minutes, then turn out onto a wire rack and cool completely.

Step 7

In a cup, mix together the brewed coffee and 1 tbsp of the coffee liqueur and keep aside.

Step 8

For the filling in a small bowl, add the mascarpone, 1/2 C. of the confectioners' sugar and 2 tbsp of the coffee liqueur and with an electric mixer set on low speed, beat till just smooth.

Step 9

Cover with plastic wrap and refrigerate.

Step 10

For the frosting in a medium bowl, add the cream, 1/4 C. of the confectioners' sugar and 2 tbsp of the coffee liqueur and with an electric mixer set on medium-high speed, beat till stiff.

Step 11

Fold 1/2 C. of the cream mixture into the filling mixture.

Step 12

For assembling, place one plain cake layer on a serving plate and with a thin skewer, poke holes in cake, about 1 inch apart.

Step 13

Place one third of the reserved coffee mixture over the cake, then spread half of the filling mixture.

Step 14

Top with the coffee-flavored cake layer and poke the holes in the cake.

Step 15

Place another third of the coffee mixture over the second layer and spread with the remaining filling.

Step 16

Top with the remaining cake layer and poke holes in the cake.

Step 17

Place the remaining coffee mixture on top.

Step 18

Spread the frosting on the sides and top of the cake.

Step 19

Place cocoa in a sieve and lightly dust over the cake and garnish with the chocolate curls.

Step 20

Refrigerate the cake for at least 30 minutes before serving.

Step 21

(To make the chocolate curls, use a vegetable peeler and run it down the edge of the chocolate bar.)

DARK CHOCOLATE CAKE

Prep Time: 30 mins **- Total Time:** 2 hrs

Servings per Recipe: 12

NUTRITIONALR VALUE

Calories528 kcal, Fat 26.4 g, Carbohydrates 66g, Protein 6.1 g, Cholesterol 63 mg, Sodium 498 mg

INGREDIENTS

- 1 (18.25 oz.) package dark chocolate cake

- 1/3 C. vegetable oil

- mix

- 1/2 C. coffee flavored liqueur

- 1 (3.9 oz.) package instant chocolate

- 2 C. semisweet chocolate chips

- pudding mix

- 1 (16 oz.) container sour cream

- 3 eggs

DIRECTIONS

Step 1

Set your oven to 350 degrees F before doing anything else and grease and flour a bundt pan.

Step 2

In a large bowl, add the pudding mix, cake mix, eggs, sour cream, oil and coffee liqueur and beat till well combined.

Step 3

Transfer the mixture into the prepared pan and cook in the oven for about 60 minutes or till a toothpick inserted in the center comes out clean.

Step 4

Cool for about 10 minutes in the pan, then turn out and cool completely on wire rack.

A SOUTHERN CAKE

Prep Time: 15 mins **- Total Time:** 8hrs 50 mins

Servings per Recipe: 12

NUTRITIONALR VALUE

Calories288 kcal, Fat 14.6 g, Carbohydrates 36.6g, Protein 3.5 g, Cholesterol 42 mg, Sodium 190 mg

INGREDIENTS

- 1 (18.25 oz.) package white cake mix

- 1 (14 oz.) can sweetened condensed milk

- 3 eggs

- 1 C. heavy whipping cream

- 1/3 C. vegetable oil

- 1 tbsp white sugar

- 1 C. water

- 1 C. flaked coconut

- 1/2 tsp coconut extract

- 1 (14 oz.) can sweetened cream of

- coconut

DIRECTIONS

Step 1

Set your oven to 350 degrees F before doing anything else and grease and flour a 13x9-inch cake pan.

Step 2

In a large bowl, add the cake mix, eggs, oil, water and coconut flavoring and beat for about 2 minutes.

Step 3

Transfer the mixture into the prepared pan and cook in the oven for about 30 minutes or till a toothpick inserted in the center comes out clean.

Step 4

In a medium bowl, add the coconut cream and sweetened condensed milk and stir till smooth.

Step 5

Remove the cake from the oven and with a fork, poke holes.

Step 6

Place the milk mixture over the cake, allowing it to soak into the cake.

Step 7

Refrigerate for several hours or overnight.

Step 8

In a large bowl, add the cream and beat till soft peaks form.

Step 9

Add the sugar and beat till stiff.

Step 10

Spread over cooled cake and serve with a sprinkling of the flaked coconut.

MOROCCAN STYLE ORANGE CAKE

Prep Time: 30 mins **- Total Time:** 2 hrs

Servings per Recipe: 12

NUTRITIONALR VALUE

Calories410 kcal, Fat 19.8 g, Carbohydrates 55g, Protein 4.2 g, Cholesterol 73 mg, Sodium 443 mg

INGREDIENTS

- 1 (18.25 oz.) package yellow cake mix

- 1 tsp lemon extract

- 1 (3 oz.) package instant lemon pudding

- 1/3 C. orange juice

- mix

- 2/3 C. white sugar

- 3/4 C. orange juice

- 1/4 C. butter

- 1/2 C. vegetable oil

- 4 eggs

DIRECTIONS

Step 1

Set your oven to 450 degrees F before doing anything else and grease and flour a bundt pan.

Step 2

In a large bowl, mix together the cake mix and pudding mix.

Step 3

Make a well in the center and add in 3/4 C. of the orange juice, oil, eggs and lemon extract and eat on low speed till well combined.

Step 4

Scrape the bowl, and now, beat on medium speed for about 4 minutes.

Step 5

Transfer the mixture into the prepared pan and cook in the oven for about 50-60 minutes or till a toothpick inserted in the center comes out clean.

Step 6

Let the cake cool in the pan for about 10 minutes, then turn out onto a wire rack and cool completely.

Step 7

In a pan, add 1/3 C. of the orange juice, sugar and butter on medium heat and cook for about 2 minutes.

Step 8

Drizzle over the cake.

HOMEMADE WEDDING CAKE

Prep Time: 10 mins - **Total Time:** 1 hr 05 mins

Servings per Recipe: 20

NUTRITIONALR VALUE

Calories211 kcal, Fat 6.6 g, Carbohydrates 35.3g, Protein 2.9 g, Cholesterol 5 mg, Sodium 275 mg

INGREDIENTS

- 1 (18.25 oz.) package white cake mix

- 1 tsp almond extract

- 1 C. all-purpose flour

- 1 tsp vanilla extract

- 1 C. white sugar

- 4 egg whites

- 3/4 tsp salt

- 1 1/3 C. water

- 1 C. sour cream

- 2 tbsp vegetable oil

DIRECTIONS

Step 1

Set your oven to 325 degrees F before doing anything else and grease and flour a 13x11-inch cake pan.

Step 2

In a bowl, mix together the white cake mix, flour, sugar, and salt.

Step 3

Add the sour cream, egg whites, vegetable oil, water, almond and vanilla extracts and beat with an electric mix on low for about 4 minutes.

Step 4

Transfer the mixture into the prepared pan and cook in the oven for about 25 minutes or till a toothpick inserted in the center comes out clean.

Step 5

Allow to cool before frosting.

STRAWBERRY PUNCH CAKE

Prep Time: 15 mins **- Total Time:** 1 hr 20 mins

Servings per Recipe: 12

NUTRITIONALR VALUE

Calories290 kcal, Fat 5 g, Carbohydrates 58.3g, Protein 3.1 g, Cholesterol 1 mg, Sodium 331 mg

INGREDIENTS

- 2 C. crushed fresh strawberries

- 1 (18 oz.) package yellow cake mix, batter

- 1 (6 oz.) package strawberry flavored Jell-

- prepared as directed on package

- O(R) mix

- 3 C. miniature marshmallows

DIRECTIONS

Step 1

Set your oven to 350 degrees F before doing anything else.

Step 2

In the bottom of a 13x9-inch baking dish, spread the crushed strawberries and sprinkle with the dry gelatin powder and then top with the mini marshmallows.

Step 3

Mix the cake mix according to the package's directions.

Step 4

Transfer the mixture into the pan over the marshmallows and cook in the oven for about 40-50 minutes or till a toothpick inserted in the center comes out clean.

CHEESECAKE JAPANESE STYLE

Prep Time: 35 mins **- Total Time:** 1 hr 40 mins

Servings per Recipe: 8

NUTRITIONALR VALUE

Calories99 kcal, Fat 5 g, Carbohydrates 10.8g, Protein 2.9 g, Cholesterol 64 mg, Sodium 51 mg

INGREDIENTS

- 1 (3 oz.) package cream cheese

- 1/3 tsp cream of tartar

- 1/4 C. milk

- 3 tbsp all-purpose flour

- 2 egg yolks

- 1 1/2 tbsp cornstarch

- 1/4 C. white sugar, divided

- 2 egg whites

DIRECTIONS

Step 1

Set your oven to 350 degrees F before doing anything else and line a 9-inch round cake pan with the parchment paper.

Step 2

In a small pan, add the cream cheese and milk on medium-low heat and cook, stirring occasionally till the cream cheese melts.

Step 3

Remove from the heat and keep aside.

Step 4

In a medium bowl, add the egg yolks and half of the sugar and with an electric mixer, beat till fluffy and light.

Step 5

Fold the cream cheese mixture into the yolks.

Step 6

Sift in the flour and cornstarch and stir till well combined.

Step 7

In another bowl, add the egg whites and cream of tartar and beat till soft peaks form.

Step 8

Slowly, add the remaining sugar and continue beating till the stiff peaks form.

Step 9

Fold the egg whites into the cream cheese mixture.

Step 10

Place the mixture into the prepared cake pan.

Step 11

Arrange the cake pan onto a baking dish and pour water into the baking dish to half way full.

Step 12

Cook in the oven for about 20 minutes.

Step 13

Now, set the oven to 300 degrees F and cook for about 15 minutes more.

Step 14

Let the cake cool before removing from the pan.

Step 15

Run a knife around the outer edge of the cake pan, and invert onto a plate to remove the cake.

Step 16

Peel off the parchment paper and invert onto a serving plate so the top of the cake is on top again.

DELIGHTFUL CHEESECAKE

Prep Time: 20 mins **- Total Time:** 1 hr 30 mins

Servings per Recipe: 12

NUTRITIONALR VALUE

Calories324 kcal, Fat 21.2 g, Carbohydrates 28.1g, Protein 5.1 g, Cholesterol 80 mg, Sodium 200 mg

INGREDIENTS

- 1 (9 inch) prepared shortbread pie crust

- 2 (8 oz.) packages cream cheese

- 1 C. white sugar

- 2 eggs

- 2 tsp vanilla extract

- 1 C. sour cream

DIRECTIONS

Step 1

Set your oven to 325 degrees F before doing anything else.

Step 2

In a bowl, add the cream cheese and sugar and beat well.

Step 3

Add the eggs one at time, beating till well combined.

Step 4

Add the vanilla and sour cream and mix, then transfer into the shortbread crust.

Step 5

Cook in the oven for about 60-70 minutes

Step 6

Run a knife around the outside edge, but leave the cake in the pan.

Step 7

Let it cool on the counter, then place in refrigerator.

Step 8

Remove from pan when completely chilled, and serve.

EXPRESSO CHEESECAKE

Prep Time: 35 mins **- Total Time:** 10hrs 03 mins

Servings per Recipe: 12

NUTRITIONALR VALUE

Calories486 kcal, Fat 35 g, Carbohydrates 37.1g, Protein 7.7 g, Cholesterol 141 mg, Sodium 363 mg

INGREDIENTS

- 2 C. graham cracker crumbs

- 1 (8 oz.) container sour cream

- 1/2 C. butter, melted

- 1/4 C. brewed espresso or strong coffee

- 2 tbsp white sugar

- 2 tsp vanilla extract

- 3 (8 oz.) packages cream cheese, softened

- pressurized whipped cream

- 1 C. white sugar

- caramel ice cream topping

- 3 eggs

DIRECTIONS

Step 1

Set your oven to 350 degrees F before doing anything else and grease a 9-inch spring form pan.

Step 2

In a bowl, mix together the graham cracker crumbs, melted butter and 2 tbsp of the sugar.

Step 3

Place the mixture into the bottom and 1-inch up the sides of an 8 inch spring form pan and press to smooth.

Step 4

Cook in the oven for about 8 minutes.

Step 5

Now, set the oven to 325 degrees F.

Step 6

In a large bowl, add the softened cream cheese and with an electric mixer and beat till fluffy.

Step 7

Slowly, add 1 C. of the sugar, beating till well combined.

Step 8

Add eggs, one at a time, beating well.

Step 9

Stir in the sour cream, espresso and vanilla.

Step 10

Transfer the mixture into the prepared pan and cook in the oven for about 65 minutes.

Step 11

Turn the oven off, partially open the door and allow the cheesecake to rest for about 15 minutes more.

Step 12

Remove from the oven, and run a knife around the edges.

Step 13

Cool the cheesecake on a wire rack at room temperature.

Step 14

Cover the spring form pan with a plastic wrap, and refrigerate to chill for about 8 hours.

Step 15

To serve, cut the cheesecake into wedges and garnish each slice with whipped cream and caramel sauce.

STYLE CHEESECAKE

Prep Time: 30 mins - **Total Time:** 1 hr 30 mins

Servings per Recipe: 12

NUTRITIONALR VALUE

Calories371 kcal, Fat 26.7 g, Carbohydrates 27.7g, Protein 6.8 g, Cholesterol 117 mg, Sodium 232 mg

INGREDIENTS

- 1 1/2 C. finely ground graham cracker

- 1 C. sour cream

- crumbs

- 3 tbsp all-purpose flour

- 2 tbsp white sugar

- 3 eggs

- 1/4 C. unsalted butter, melted

- 3/4 C. key lime juice

- 1 1/4 lb. cream cheese, softened

- 1 tsp vanilla extract

- 3/4 C. white sugar

DIRECTIONS

Step 1

Set your oven to 375 degrees F before doing anything else.

Step 2

For crust in a bowl mix together the graham cracker crumbs and 2 tbsp of the sugar.

Step 3

Add the butter and stir till well combined.

Step 4

Place the mixture into the bottom and 1 3/4-inch up the sides of an 8 inch spring form pan and press to smooth.

Step 5

Cook in the oven for about 8 minutes.

Step 6

Transfer the pan to a rack and cool.

Step 7

In a large add the cream cheese and 3/4 C. sugar and with an electric mixer, beat till smooth.

Step 8

Add the eggs, one at a time, beating well.

Step 9

Add the sour cream, flour, lime juice and vanilla and beat till smooth.

Step 10

Place the filling over the crust and cook in the oven for about 15 minutes.

Step 11

Now, set the oven to 250 degrees F and cook for about 50-55 minutes more.

Step 12

Let the cheesecake cool on a rack, then refrigerate, covered to chill for overnight.

Step 13

Remove the cheesecake from the pan and transfer it to a cake stand.

FAMOUS CHEESECAKE (RHUBARB)

Prep Time: 10 mins - **Total Time:** 55 mins

Servings per Recipe: 8

NUTRITIONALR VALUE

Calories421 kcal, Carbohydrates 44.8 g, Cholesterol 90 mg, Fat 24.5 g , Fiber 1.7 g, Protein 6.7 g, Sodium 234 mg

INGREDIENTS

- 1 (9 inch) unbaked pie shell

- 1 (8 oz) container sour cream

- 3 C. chopped fresh rhubarb

- 2 tbsps white sugar

- 1/2 C. white sugar

- 1 tsp vanilla extract

- 3 tbsps all-purpose flour

- 1 (8 oz) package cream cheese, softened

- 1/2 C. white sugar

- 2 eggs

DIRECTIONS

Step 1

Set your oven at 400 degrees before doing anything else.

Step 2

Coat rhubarb with a mixture of sugar and flour very thoroughly before cooking this in the preheated oven for about 15 minutes

Step 3

Turn down the temperature to 350 degrees after removing rhubarb.

Step 4

Pour a mixture of eggs, sugar and cream cheese over rhubarb.

Step 5

Bake this in the preheated oven for about 30 minutes before pouring a mixture of sour cream, sugar and vanilla over it.

Step 6

Cool it down by placing it in the refrigerator.

Step 7

Serve.

SPANISH BERRY CHEESECAKE

Prep Time: 30 mins - **Total Time:** 1hr 30 mins

Servings per Recipe: 10

NUTRITIONALR VALUE

Calories490 kcal, Fat 30 g, Carbohydrates 41.4g, Protein 10 g, Cholesterol 127 mg, Sodium 368 mg

INGREDIENTS

- 40 vanilla wafers, crushed

- 1 C. cottage cheese, creamed

- 6 tbsp butter, melted

- 1/4 C. cherry brandy

- 2 (8 oz.) packages cream cheese, softened

- 3 eggs

- 3/4 C. white sugar

- 3 1/2 C. fresh blackberries

- 2 tbsp all-purpose flour

- 1 tbsp cherry brandy

- 2 tsp vanilla extract

- 1 tbsp white sugar

DIRECTIONS

Step 1

Set your oven to 375 degrees F before doing anything else.

Step 2

In a medium bowl, mix together the vanilla wafer crumbs and butter.

Step 3

Place the mixture into the bottom and 1 3/4-inch up the sides of an 8 inch spring form pan and press to smooth.

Step 4

In another large bowl, add the cream cheese, 3/4 C. of the sugar, flour and vanilla and with an electric mixer, beat on low speed till smooth.

Step 5

In a blender, place the cottage cheese and pulse till smooth.

Step 6

Add the cottage cheese and 1/4 C. of the cherry brandy into the cream cheese mixture and mix well.

Step 7

Add the eggs and beat on low speed till just combined.

Step 8

Place half of the cheese mixture into the crust-lined pan.

Step 9

Spread 1 C. of the blackberries on top.

Step 10

Repeat the layers once.

Step 11

Arrange the spring form pan in a shallow baking pan and cook in the oven for about 40-45 minutes.

Step 12

Cool on a wire rack for about 15 minutes.

Step 13

Loosen the sides and cool completely on wire rack.

Step 14

Refrigerate, covered to chill for at least 4 hours or until ready to serve.

Step 15

For topping, in a medium bowl mix together the remaining 2 C. of the blackberries, 1 tbsp of the cherry brandy, and 1 tbsp of the sugar.

Step 16

Cover the mixture and refrigerate to chill for up to 2 hours.

Step 17

While serving, cut the cheesecake into wedges and top each serving with fruit topping.

COOKIES I

Prep Time: 15 mins **- Total Time:** 4 hrs 15 mins

Servings per Recipe: 8

NUTRITIONALR VALUE

Calories546 kcal, Carbohydrates 55.3 g, Cholesterol 90 mg, Fat 35.3 g , Fiber 2 g, Protein 6.5 g, Sodium 228 mg

INGREDIENTS

- 2 (8 oz) packages cream cheese

- cookies with chocolate filling (eg Pepperidge 1 C. white sugar

- Farm Milano)

- 1 pint heavy cream

- 1 (21 oz) can raspberry pie filling

- 4 (7 oz) packages oval butter sandwich

DIRECTIONS

Step 1

Combine cream cheese and sugar before adding thoroughly whipped cream into it.

Step 2

Place cookies at the bottom and sides of a spring form pan before pouring half of your cream cheese mixture over it.

Step 3

Spread raspberry filling evenly before placing cookies and repeating the step.

Step 4

Refrigerate it for at least 4 hours before serving.

PINEAPPLE COOKIES

Prep Time: 10 mins **- Total Time:** 2 hrs 10 min

Servings per Recipe: 8

NUTRITIONALR VALUE

Calories421 kcal, Carbohydrates 44.8 g, Cholesterol 90 mg, Fat 24.5 g , Fiber 1.7 g, Protein 6.7 g, Sodium 234 mg

INGREDIENTS

- 1 (8 oz) package cream cheese, softened

- 1 3/4 C. frozen whipped topping, thawed

- 1/2 C. white sugar

- 1 (9 inch) prepared graham cracker crust

- 2 (15 oz) cans crushed pineapple,

- drained

DIRECTIONS

Step 1

Add 1 can of pineapple and whipped topping into a mixture of cream cheese and sugar.

Step 2

Mix it thoroughly before pouring into your crust and topping it with another can of pineapple.

Step 3

Refrigerate it for at least 2 hours.

CINNAMON VANILLA COOKIES

Prep Time: 10 mins **- Total Time:** 40 mins

Servings per Recipe: 8

NUTRITIONALR VALUE

Calories483 kcal, Carbohydrates 44.9 g, Cholesterol 61 mg, Fat 30.7 g , Fiber 0.3 g, Protein 6.3 g, Sodium 532 mg

INGREDIENTS

- 2 (10 oz) cans refrigerated crescent dinner 1/2 C. butter, melted rolls

- 1/2 C. white sugar

- 2 (8 oz) packages cream cheese, softened

- 1 tbsp ground cinnamon

- 1 C. white sugar

- 1 tbsp vanilla extract

DIRECTIONS

Step 1

Set your oven at 350 degrees before doing anything else.

Step 2

Put flattened out crescent roll dough in a baking pan before spreading a mixture of cream cheese, vanilla and sugar over it.

Step 3

Wrap it up with the remaining dough before spreading melted butter on top.

Step 4

Bake this in the preheated oven for about 30 minutes

Step 5

Refrigerate it for a couple of hours.

Step 6

Serve.

BROWN SUGAR, PECANS AND PUMPKIN

Prep Time: 15 mins- **Total Time:** 1 hr

Servings per Recipe: 12

NUTRITIONALR VALUE

Calories340 kcal, Carbohydrates 36.8 gCookies, Cholesterol 68 mg, Fat 20.3 g , Fiber 1.2 g, Protein 4.5 g, Sodium 221 mg

INGREDIENTS

- 1/2 C. chopped pecans
- 2 eggs
- 1/4 C. packed brown sugar
- 3/4 C. pumpkin butter
- 2 tbsps butter, softened
- 1 (9 inch) prepared graham cracker crust
- 1 (8 oz) package cream cheese, softened
- 1/3 C. packed brown sugar

DIRECTIONS

Step 1

Set your oven at 350 degrees before doing anything else.

Step 2

Add brown sugar, eggs and pumpkin butter into some finely whisked cream cheese, while beating the mixture very thoroughly after every inclusion.

Step 3

Bake this in the preheated oven for about 40 minutes

Step 4

Now spread a finely combined mixture of brown sugar, butter and pecans over this pie before baking it for another 40 minutes.

Step 5

Refrigerate it for at least 4 hours.

Step 6

Serve.

THE "PERFECT" QUICHE CRUST

Prep Time: 10 mins **- Total Time:** 10 mins

Servings per Recipe: 6

NUTRITIONALR VALUE

Calories178 kcal, Carbohydrates 12 g, Cholesterol 35 mg, Fat 13.2 g , Fiber 0.4 g, Protein 2.9 g, Sodium 111 mg

INGREDIENTS

- 3/4 cup all-purpose flour

- 5 tsps cold water

- 6 tbsps cold butter, cut into small pieces

- 1/4 cup shredded Cheddar cheese

DIRECTIONS

Step 1

Preheat your oven at 350 degrees F and put some oil over the quiche dish.

Step 2

Combine flour and butter in a bowl very thoroughly before adding grated cheese.

Step 3

Add water spoon after spoon until you can form a ball out of it.

Step 4

Wrap this dough with plastic wrap before refrigerating it for at least thirty minutes.

Step 5

Roll this dough and put this in the quiche dish.

Step 6

Bake in the preheated oven for about 10 minutes before filling it with quiche custard of your choice.

AUTUMN ACORN QUICHE

Prep Time: 15 mins - **Total Time:** 1 hr 30 mins

Servings per Recipe: 6

NUTRITIONALR VALUE

Calories165 kcal, Carbohydrates 20 g, Cholesterol 142 mg, Fat 4.8 g , Fiber 2.9 g, Protein 12.6 g, Sodium 69 mg

INGREDIENTS

- 2 acorn squash

- 1 tbsp pumpkin pie spice

- 1 red onion, chopped

- salt to taste

- 1 cup chopped cooked turkey

- 4 eggs

DIRECTIONS

Step 1

Preheat your oven at 350 degrees F and put some oil over the quiche dish.

Step 2

Put squash into a baking dish and then bake it in the preheated oven for one full hour before cutting this in half, removing seeds and scrapping the meat out in a bowl.

Step 3

Combine squash, turkey, eggs, pumpkin pie spice, onion and salt together in a medium sized bowl before pouring this mixture into the quiche dish **Step 4**

Bake in the preheated oven for about 45 minutes or until the top of the quiche is golden brown in color.

VEGGIE CHEESE BITES

Prep Time: 15 mins **- Total Time:** 1 hr

Servings per Recipe: 6

NUTRITIONALR VALUE

Calories 530 kcal, Carbohydrates 23.8 g, Cholesterol

196 mg, Fat 36.5 g , Fiber 3.4 g, Protein 28.2 g, Sodium 1068 mg

INGREDIENTS

- 1/4 cup butter

- 1 cup all-purpose flour

- 2 (10 ounce) packages frozen broccoli

- 3 eggs

- florets, thawed and drained

- 1 tsp baking powder

- 1 pound shredded sharp Cheddar cheese

- 1 tsp salt

- 1 cup milk

- ground black pepper to taste

DIRECTIONS

Step 1

Preheat your oven at 350 degrees F and put some oil over the quiche dish.

Step 2

Combine broccoli, milk, flour, eggs, baking powder, salt, Cheddar cheese and black pepper in medium sized bowl.

Step 3

Pour this mixture in the quiche dish over melted butter.

Step 4

Bake in the preheated oven for about 45 minutes or until the top of the quiche is golden brown in color.

Step 5

Serve.

NUTTY HONEY QUICHE

Prep Time: 20 mins - **Total Time:** 1 hr

Servings per Recipe: 8

NUTRITIONALR VALUE

Calories586 kcal, Fat 47.4 g, Carbohydrates 34.1g, Protein 10.2 g, Cholesterol 175 mg, Sodium 468 mg

INGREDIENTS

- 1/2 C. butter

- 1/2 tsp nutmeg

- 1 C. sliced carrots

- 1/2 tsp salt

- 1 C. cashews

- 3/4 C. shredded Cheddar cheese

- 1/2 C. honey

- 1 (9 in.) pie crust

- 3 eggs

- 1 1/2 C. heavy cream

DIRECTIONS

Step 1

Set your oven to 350 degrees before doing anything else.

Step 2

Stir fry your cashews and carrots in melted butter until the carrots are soft.

Step 3

Now add in your honey, stir the mix, and shut the heat.

Step 4

Get a bowl, combine: salt, eggs, nutmeg, and heavy cream.

Step 5

Layer your cheese into the pie dish and then place the cashew mix on top before pouring in the cream mix.

Step 6

Cook everything in the oven for 38 mins.

Step 7

Enjoy.

NUTTY TANGY CHICKEN QUICHE

Prep Time: 20 mins - **Total Time:** 1 hr 10 mins

Servings per Recipe: 8

NUTRITIONALR VALUE

Calories339 kcal, Fat 23 g, Carbohydrates 15.5g, Protein 18 g, Cholesterol 92 mg, Sodium 237 mg

INGREDIENTS

- 1 C. diced, cooked chicken

- 1 (9 in.) unbaked deep-dish pastry shell

- 1 C. shredded Swiss cheese

- 2 eggs, beaten

- 1/4 C. diced onion

- 1 C. 2% milk

- 1 tbsp all-purpose flour

- 1/2 tsp brown mustard

- 1/2 C. diced pecans

DIRECTIONS

Step 1

Set your oven to 325 degrees before doing anything else.

Step 2

Get a bowl, combine: 1/4 C. pecans, chicken, flour, cheese, and onions. Enter this into your pie.

Step 3

Get a 2nd bowl, combine: mustard, the rest of the pecans, milk, and eggs. Layer this mix over the chicken mix in the pie crust and cook everything in the oven for 55 mins.

Step 4

Enjoy.

MEXICAN STYLE QUICHE

Prep Time: 15 mins **- Total Time:** 1 hr 20 mins

Servings per Recipe: 8

NUTRITIONALR VALUE

Calories520 kcal, Fat 36.4 g, Carbohydrates 23.1g, Protein 25.2 g, Cholesterol 208 mg, Sodium 1196 mg

INGREDIENTS

- 1 (9 in.) unbaked deep-dish pie crust

- 2 C. shredded Mexican cheese blend,

- 10 oz. chorizo sausage

- divided

- 6 eggs

- 1 (15 oz.) can refried beans

- 1/4 C. milk

- 1 (10 oz.) can diced tomatoes

- with green chili peppers (such as

- RO*TEL(R)), drained

DIRECTIONS

Step 1

Layer your pie crust into a pie dish and then set your oven to 400 degrees before doing anything else.

Step 2

Stir fry your chorizo for 7 mins then break it into pieces.

Step 3

Get a bowl, combine: milk and eggs. Then add in half of the cheese, the chili pepper, and the tomatoes. Stir everything together.

Step 4

Layer your beans into the pie crust and evenly distribute them.

Step 5

Now add in the chorizo and the egg mix. Top the quiche with the rest of the cheese.

Step 6

Cook the quiche in the oven for 50 mins.

Step 7

Enjoy.

A QUICHE OF MUSHROOMS AND SPINACH

Prep Time: 15 mins - **Total Time:** 50 mins

Servings per Recipe: 9

NUTRITIONALR VALUE

Calories325 kcal, Carbohydrates 10.8 g, Cholesterol 139 mg, Fat 22.5 g , Fiber 2.3 g, Protein 20.9 g, Sodium 806 mg

INGREDIENTS

- 6 slices bacon

- 2 cups chopped fresh mushrooms

- 4 eggs, beaten

- 1/2 cup chopped onions

- 1 1/2 cups light cream

- 1 cup shredded Swiss cheese

- 1/4 tsp ground nutmeg

- 1 cup shredded Cheddar cheese

- 1/2 tsp salt

- 1 (9 inch) deep dish pie crust

- 1/2 tsp pepper

- 2 cups chopped fresh spinach

DIRECTIONS

Step 1

Preheat your oven at 400 degrees F and put some oil over the quiche dish.

Step 2

Cook bacon over medium heat until brown and then crumble it after draining.

Step 3

Mix eggs, pepper, cream, salt, nutmeg, bacon, spinach, mushrooms, 3/4 cup Swiss cheese, 3/4 cup Cheddar cheese and onions in a bowl very thoroughly.

Step 4

Pour this mixture over the pie crust and add some cheese.

Step 5

Bake in the preheated oven for about 35 minutes or until the top of the quiche is golden brown in color.

THE SIMPLEST ZUCCHINI QUICHE I

Prep Time: 15 mins **- Total Time:** 45 mins

Servings per Recipe: 9

NUTRITIONALR VALUE

Calories314 kcal, Carbohydrates 15.7 g, Cholesterol 188 mg, Fat 22 g , Fiber 1.6 g, Protein 13.6 g, Sodium 364 mg

INGREDIENTS

- 2 cups grated zucchini

- 1 (9 inch) pie shell, unbaked

- 6 eggs, beaten

- 1 cup shredded Cheddar cheese

DIRECTIONS

Step 1

Preheat your oven at 350 degrees F and put some oil over the quiche dish.

Step 2

Put zucchini evenly in quiche dish before adding eggs and some cheddar cheese.

Step 3

Bake in the preheated oven for about 30 minutes or until the top of the quiche is golden brown in color.

A QUICHE OF CHILI'S AND SPINACH

Prep Time: 10 mins **- Total Time:** 1 hr

Servings per Recipe: 18

NUTRITIONALR VALUE

Calories324 kcal, Carbohydrates 16.3 g, Cholesterol 173 mg, Fat 22.9 g , Fiber 1.6 g, Protein 14 g, Sodium 786 mg

INGREDIENTS

- 1/2 cup all-purpose flour

- 1 (10 ounce) package frozen chopped spinach, 1 tsp baking powder

- thawed and drained

- 1 tsp salt

- 2 (4 ounce) cans chopped green chilies

- 12 eggs

- 1/2 cup melted butter

- 1 (8 ounce) package shredded Colby-

- 2 (9 inch) unbaked pie crusts

- Monterey Jack cheese

- 2 cups small curd cottage cheese

DIRECTIONS

Step 1

Preheat your oven at 400 degrees F and put some oil over the quiche dish before setting aside a mixture of salt, flour and baking powder.

Step 2

Whisk eggs and flour mixture together thoroughly before adding Colby-Monterey Jack cheese, spinach, green chills, cottage cheese and melted butter into it.

Step 3

Pour this mixture evenly into the quiche dishes.

Step 4

Bake in the preheated oven for about 15 minutes before turning the heat down to 350 Degrees F and baking for another 40 minutes or until the top of the quiche is golden brown in color.

CRAB QUICHE I

Prep Time: 10 mins **- Total Time:** 1 hr

Servings per Recipe: 6

NUTRITIONALR VALUE

Calories326 kcal, Carbohydrates 14.3 g, Cholesterol 83 mg, Fat 24.8 g , Fiber 1 g, Protein 11.8 g, Sodium 308 mg

INGREDIENTS

- 1/2 cup mayonnaise

- 1 cup diced Swiss cheese

- 2 tbsps all-purpose flour

- 1/2 cup chopped green onions

- 2 eggs, beaten

- 1 (9 inch) unbaked pie crust

- 1/2 cup milk

- 1 cup crab meat

DIRECTIONS

Step 1

Preheat your oven at 350 degrees F and put some oil over the quiche dish.

Step 2

Whisk eggs, milk, mayonnaise, crab, flour, onion and cheese very thoroughly.

Step 3

Pour this mixture in the quiche dish.

Step 4

Bake in the preheated oven for about 30 minutes or until the top of the quiche is golden brown in color.

A QUICHE OF PARMESAN

Prep Time: 10 mins **- Total Time:** 1 hr

Servings per Recipe: 10

NUTRITIONALR VALUE

Calories371 kcal, Carbohydrates 12.5 g, Cholesterol 161 mg, Fat 26.6 g , Fiber 1.3 g, Protein 21 g, Sodium 797 mg

INGREDIENTS

- 2 cups milk

- 1 (10 ounce) package chopped frozen broccoli, 4 eggs

- thawed and drained

- 3/4 cup biscuit baking mix

- 1 cup cubed cooked ham

- 1/4 cup butter, softened

- 8 ounces shredded Cheddar cheese

- 1 cup grated Parmesan cheese

DIRECTIONS

Step 1

Preheat your oven to 375 degrees F and put some oil over the quiche dish.

Step 2

Now mix milk, eggs, parmesan cheese, baking mix and some butter in a bowl and then add broccoli, cheddar cheese and ham.

Step 3

Mix thoroughly and bake in the preheated oven for about 50 minutes or until the top of the quiche is golden brown in color.

TRADITIONAL SCOTTISH BISCUITS

Prep Time: 30 mins **- Total Time:** 40 mins

Servings per Recipe: 18

NUTRITIONALR VALUE

Calories322 kcal, Fat 11.1 g, Carbohydrates 54.5g, Protein 2.5 g, Cholesterol 48 mg, Sodium 155 mg

INGREDIENTS

- 1/2 C. butter, softened

- 1/8 tsp salt

- 1/2 C. white sugar

- 3 C. sifted confectioners' sugar

- 2 eggs

- 1/4 C. milk, or as needed

- 2 C. all-purpose flour

- 1 1/2 tsp vanilla extract

- 1 tbsp baking powder

- 1 C. strawberry jam

- 1 tbsp allspice

- 1 (10 oz.) jar maraschino cherries, drained

- 1 tbsp ground cinnamon

- 1/2 C. butter, softened

DIRECTIONS

Step 1

Set your oven to 350 degrees F before doing anything else.

Step 2

In a large bowl add the 1/2 C. of the butter and white sugar and beat till smooth.

Step 3

Add the eggs one a time, mixing till well combine.

Step 4

In another bowl, mix together the flour, baking powder, allspice and cinnamon.

Step 5

Add the flour mixture into the butter mixture and mix till a stiff dough forms.

Step 6

Place the dough onto a lightly floured surface and roll into 1/8-1/4-inch thickness.

Step 7

With a biscuit cutter, cut into circles and place onto ungreased baking sheets about 2 inches apart.

Step 8

Cook in the oven for about 10 minutes.

Step 9

Cool cookies on wire racks for at least 15 minutes.

Step 10

Meanwhile for the frosting in a small bowl, add the butter and salt and beat till soft.

Step 11

Slowly, add the confectioners' sugar and vanilla until and mix till smooth and light.

Step 12

Spread the strawberry jam over the one side of a cookie and top with another cookie to make a jam sandwich.

Step 13

Spread frosting on top and place a maraschino cherry half in the center.

Step 14

Repeat with the remaining cookies.

BEST ARROWROOT BISCUITS

Prep Time: 15 mins **- Total Time:** 1 hr

Servings per Recipe: 18

NUTRITIONALR VALUE

Calories86 kcal, Fat 2.9 g, Carbohydrates 14.1g, Protein 1.1 g, Cholesterol 17 mg, Sodium 68 mg

INGREDIENTS

- 1/4 C. butter, softened
- 1/2 C. arrowroot flour
- 1/2 C. white sugar
- 1/2 tsp baking powder
- 1 egg
- 1/4 tsp salt
- 1/2 tsp vanilla extract
- 1 C. all-purpose flour

DIRECTIONS

Step 1

Set your oven to 350 degrees F before doing anything else and line the cookie sheets with the parchment papers.

Step 2

In a bowl, add the butter and sugar and beat till just smooth.

Step 3

Add the egg and vanilla and beat well.

Step 4

In another bowl, mix together the flour, arrowroot flour, baking powder and salt.

Step 5

Add the flour mixture into the butter mixture and mix well.

Step 6

Divide dough in 2 portions.

Step 7

On a lightly floured surface, roll both the dough portions separately into 1/8-inch thickness and cut into 2 1/2-inch rounds.

Step 8

Place the rounds onto the prepared cookie sheets and with a fork, prick them.

Step 9

Cook in the oven for about 8-10 minutes.

AUSTRALIAN BISCUITS

Prep Time: 15 mins **- Total Time:** 30 mins

Servings per Recipe: 22

NUTRITIONALR VALUE

Calories90 kcal, Fat 5.1 g, Carbohydrates 10.6g, Protein 0.8 g, Cholesterol 11 mg, Sodium 49 mg

INGREDIENTS

- 3/4 C. rolled oats

- 2 tbsp boiling water

- 3/4 C. sweetened flaked coconut

- 1/2 C. butter, melted

- 1/2 C. all-purpose flour

- 1 tbsp golden syrup

- 1/2 C. white sugar

- 1/2 tsp baking powder

DIRECTIONS

Step 1

Set your oven to 350 degrees F before doing anything else and lightly, grease the cookie sheets.

Step 2

In a bowl, mix together the flour, oats, coconut and sugar.

Step 3

In another bowl, dissolve the baking powder in the boiling water.

Step 4

Add the butter and golden syrup and mix well.

Step 5

Add the butter mixture into the oat mixture and mix till a dough forms.

Step 6

With a tbsp, place the dough onto the prepared cookie sheets about 2 inches apart and with a lightly floured fork, flatten the biscuits.

Step 7

Cook in the oven for about 15 minutes.

GOOEY ARROWROOT BISCUITS

Prep Time: 15 mins - **Total Time:** 30 mins

Servings per Recipe: 8

NUTRITIONALR VALUE

Calories560 kcal, Fat 27.7 g, Carbohydrates 86.3g, Protein 8.7 g, Cholesterol 19 mg, Sodium 609 mg

INGREDIENTS

- 1 1/4 C. Reduced Fat Bisquick(R)

- 3 tbsp melted butter

- 1 C. whole wheat baking mix

- 1/2 C. confectioners' sugar

- 2/3 C. buttermilk

- 1 tbsp melted butter

- 2 C. HERSHEY(R)'S Cinnamon Chips

- 1 tbsp water

- 1 C. cinnamon coated raisins

DIRECTIONS

Step 1

Set your oven to 425 degrees F before doing anything else.

Step 2

In a food processor, add the cinnamon chips and pulse till grounded roughly.

Step 3

Transfer 1/2 of the chips into a bowl.

Step 4

Continue to pulse the remaining chips till ground finely.

Step 5

In a large bowl, mix together the baking mixes, 1 C. of the roughly grounded cinnamon chips and raisins.

Step 6

Make a well in the center of the mixture and add the buttermilk, and stir till the dough comes together.

Step 7

Place the dough onto a lightly floured smooth surface and knead gently for about 1 minute.

Step 8

Flatten the dough to an 8x10-inch rectangle and coat with the melted butter.

Step 9

Sprinkle with the finely ground cinnamon chips evenly.

Step 10

Starting from one long side, roll up the dough and pinch seams and ends to seal.

Step 11

Cut the roll crosswise into 8 equal slices and place in a 13x9-inch ungreased baking dish.

Step 12

Cook in the oven for about 12 minutes.

Step 13

In a bowl, add the confectioners' sugar, 1 tbsp of the melted butter and water and mix till smooth.

Step 14

Drizzle glaze over the hot biscuits.

OLD-FASHIONED BISCUITS

Prep Time: 10 mins **- Total Time:** 20 mins

Servings per Recipe: 12

NUTRITIONALR VALUE

Calories114 kcal, Fat 4.1 g, Carbohydrates 16.6g, Protein 2.4 g, Cholesterol 2 mg, Sodium 398 mg

INGREDIENTS

- 2 1/2 C. buttermilk baking mix
- 1 tsp baking powder
- 1 pinch salt
- 2/3 C. milk
- 1/2 tbsp malt vinegar

DIRECTIONS

Step 1

Set your oven to 450 degrees F before doing anything else and lightly, grease 2 cookie sheets.

Step 2

In a large bowl, mix together the baking mix, baking powder and salt.

Step 3

Add the milk and vinegar and mix till a loose dough forms.

Step 4

Place the dough onto a lightly floured surface and knead for about 10 times.

Step 5

Divide the dough into 12 equal pieces and place on prepared baking sheets.

Step 6

Cook in the oven for about 8-10 minutes

AMERICAN STYLE BISCUITS

Prep Time: 25 mins **- Total Time:** 40 mins

Servings per Recipe: 24

NUTRITIONALR VALUE

Calories67 kcal, Fat 2.9 g, Carbohydrates 8.9g, Protein 1.2 g, Cholesterol

4 mg, Sodium 31 mg

INGREDIENTS

- 2 C. all-purpose flour
- 1/4 C. lard, chilled and cut into small pieces 1/4 tsp salt
- 1/3 C. light cream
- 1/4 tsp baking powder
- 2 tbsp cold water
- 1 1/2 tbsp white sugar

DIRECTIONS

Step 1

Set your oven to 450 degrees F before doing anything else and lightly, grease the cookie sheets.

Step 2

In a bowl, sift together the flour, baking powder, sugar and salt.

Step 3

With a fork cut the lard into the flour mixture and mix till a coarse meal forms.

Step 4

Slowly add the cream and with a wooden spoon, mix till the dough forms into a ball. (Add water if needed.)

Step 5

Place the dough onto a smooth surface and knead slightly.

Step 6

With a rolling pin, roll the dough a few times to form it into a rough rectangle.

Step 7

Fold the dough over, and then roll it again and repeat this process for about 15 minutes.

Step 8

Roll the dough into 1/4-inch thickness and cut into 2-inch rounds.

Step 9

With a fork, prick the top a few times and place onto the prepared cookie sheets.

Step 10

Cook in the oven for about 15 minutes.

SIMPLE BUTTER MILK BISCUITS

Prep Time: 15 mins **- Total Time:** 25 mins

Servings per Recipe: 12

NUTRITIONALR VALUE

Calories147 kcal, Fat 8 g, Carbohydrates 16.1g, Protein 2.6 g, Cholesterol 21 mg, Sodium 333 mg

INGREDIENTS

- 2 C. self-rising flour

- 1/2 C. butter

- 2/3 C. buttermilk

DIRECTIONS

Step 1

Set your oven to 450 degrees F before doing anything else and lightly, grease a cookie sheet.

Step 2

In a large bowl, add the flour and with a pastry cutter, cut the butter and mix till a coarse crumb forms.

Step 3

Slowly, add the buttermilk and mix till well combined.

Step 4

With a round tbsp, place the mixture onto the prepared cookie sheet.

Step 5

Cook in the oven for about 10 minutes.

9 7 9 8 4 3 6 7 2 6 8 4 7